ANKYLOSAURUS

A Buddy Book
by
Michael P. Goecke

ABDO
Publishing Company

VISIT US AT
www.abdopub.com

Published by ABDO Publishing Company, 4940 Viking Drive, Edina, Minnesota 55435. Copyright © 2002 by Abdo Consulting Group, Inc. International copyrights reserved in all countries. No part of this book may be reproduced in any form without written permission from the publisher.

Printed in the United States.

Edited by: Christy DeVillier
Contributing editor: Matt Ray
Graphic Design: Denise Esner, Maria Hosley
Cover Art: Maria Hosley, title page
Interior Photos/Illustrations: pages 5, 8, 9, 21 & 27: Maria Hosley; page11: M. Shiraishi ©1999 All Rights Reserved; page 15: ©Douglas Henderson from *Riddle of the Dinosaur* by John Noble Wilford, published by Knopf; page 17: Deborah Coldiron; page 19: Rich Penny, www.dinosaur-man.com; page 20: Joe Tucciarone; page 24: Denise Esner.

Library of Congress Cataloging-in-Publication Data

Goecke, Michael P., 1968-
    Ankylosaurus/Michael P. Goecke.
      p. cm. – (Dinosaurs set II)
    Includes index.
    Summary: Describes the physical characteristics and behavior of the armored dinosaur Ankylosaurus.
    ISBN 1-57765-637-7
    1. Ankylosaurus—Juvenile literature. [1. Ankylosaurus. 2. Dinosaurs.] I. Title.

QE862.O65 G59 2002
567.915—dc21

2001027930

TABLE OF CONTENTS

What Were They?..4

How Did They Move?..8

Why Was It Special?..10

Land Of The Ankylosaurus 12

Who Else Lived There? 14

What Did They Eat? 16

Who Were Their Enemies? 18

The Family Tree 22

Discovery 26

Where Are They Today?......................................28

Fun Dinosaur Web Sites......................................30

Important Words 31

Index 32

WHAT WERE THEY?

The Ankylosaurus was a plant-eating dinosaur. It lived about 70 million years ago. That was during the late Cretaceous period.

The Ankylosaurus was 25 feet (8 m) long. It was only about four feet (one m) tall. It looked a little like a giant, flat turtle.

The Ankylosaurus weighed about 10,000 pounds (4,536 kg). That is as big as a hippopotamus.

How did they move?

The Ankylosaurus walked on all four legs. These legs were short and strong. This dinosaur did not move very fast.

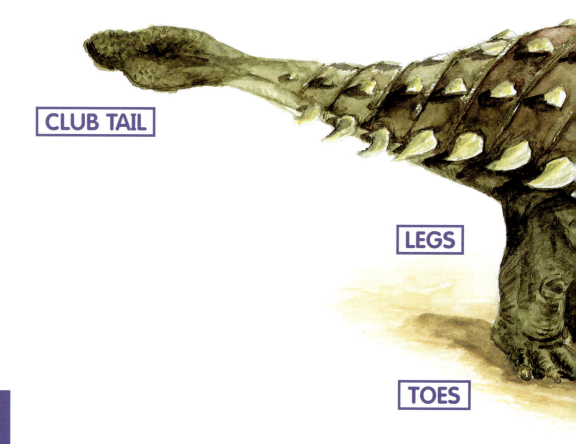

CLUB TAIL

LEGS

TOES

Its back legs were longer than its front legs. This helped the Ankylosaurus hold its round belly off the ground. Its head stayed close to the ground.

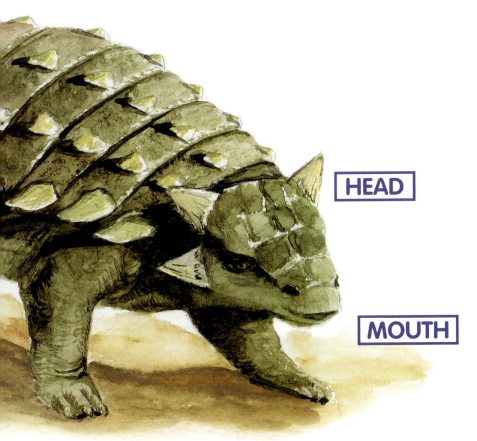

HEAD

MOUTH

WHY WAS IT SPECIAL?

The Ankylosaurus had armor, or hard plates. These plates covered the head, back, tail, and legs. Even its eyelids had armor plating. Only its belly did not have armor.

Hard plates covered the Ankylosaurus.

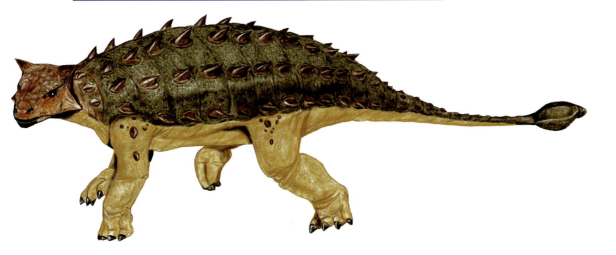

LAND OF THE ANKYLOSAURUS

The Ankylosaurus lived in North America and South America. North America and South America are continents. These continents looked different in the late Cretaceous period. North America and South America were the same land mass. Shallow seas circled this huge land mass.

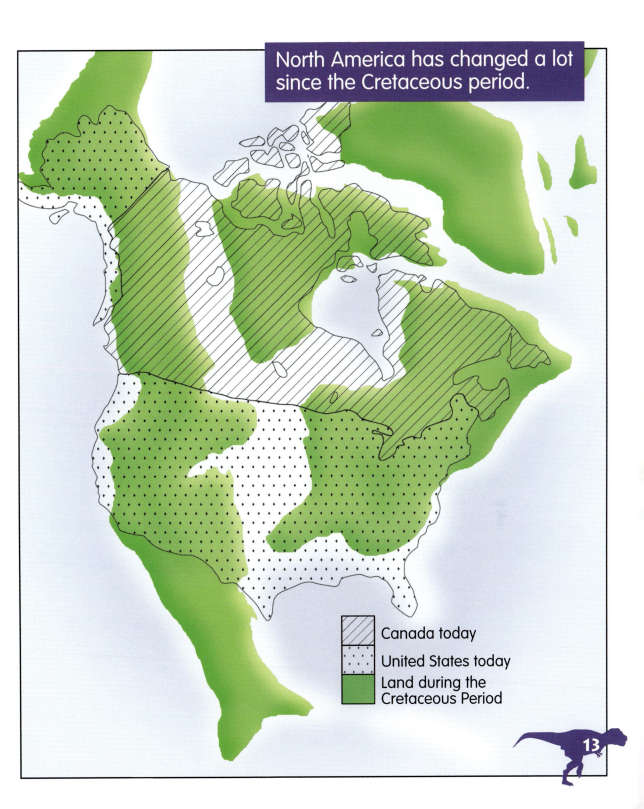

WHO ELSE LIVED THERE?

The Ankylosaurus lived among many plant-eating dinosaurs. One was the Triceratops. The Triceratops had two horns above each eye. A third horn sat on its nose. This dinosaur did not have as much armor as the Ankylosaurus. Yet, it had a hard plate on its head. We call this plate a frill.

The Triceratops

WHAT DID THEY EAT?

The Ankylosaurus gathered plants with a beak. It had teeth, too. But these teeth were not good for chewing.

How did the Ankylosaurus break up its food? Maybe this happened in the belly. This plant-eater may have had a powerful stomach. A powerful stomach could break up something hard like wood.

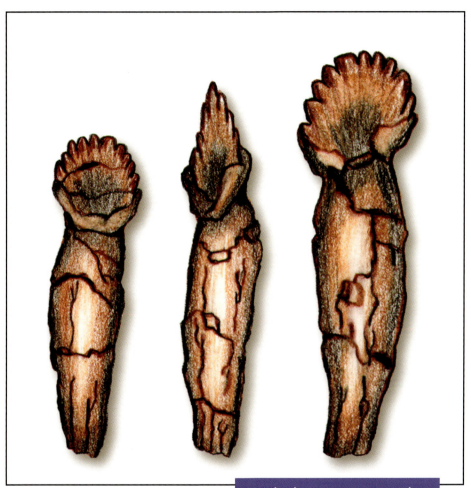

Ankylosaurus teeth

WHO WERE THEIR ENEMIES?

The Tyrannosaurus rex was a big, meat-eating dinosaur. It had sharp teeth and claws. The T. rex was a fast and powerful hunter. It may have hunted the Ankylosaurus.

The T. rex may have hunted the Ankylosaurus.

The Ankylosaurus's armor helped to keep it safe.

How did the Ankylosaurus guard itself from the big T. rex? Its tough armor helped. Maybe the Ankylosaurus used its special tail, too. This tail was big on the end. We call it a club tail. Maybe the Ankylosaurus hit enemies with its club tail.

The Ankylosaurus had a club tail.

THE FAMILY TREE

The Ankylosaurus was an ankylosaur. Ankylosaur dinosaurs had armor and horns. Other ankylosaur dinosaurs were the Panoplosaurus and the Edmontonia. These ankylosaurs were smaller than the Ankylosaurus.

The Ankylosaurus was the biggest ankylosaur.

Ankylosaurus

Edmontonia

Panoplosaurus

The Panoplosaurus

There were two groups of ankylosaurs. One group was the ankylosaurids. The Ankylosaurus belonged to the ankylosaurids. The ankylosaurids had club tails and wide heads.

The second group of ankylosaurs was the nodosaurids. The nodosaurids did not have club tails. The nodosaurids had spikes on their sides. The Panoplosaurus and the Edmontonia were nodosaurid dinosaurs.

Discovery

Sometimes, people find dinosaur footprints. These footprints are fossils. We call them trackways. In 1996, paleontologists found Ankylosaurus trackways near Sucre, Bolivia. These trackways helped people understand how the Ankylosaurus walked. The Ankylosaurus got its name from paleontologist Barnum Brown.

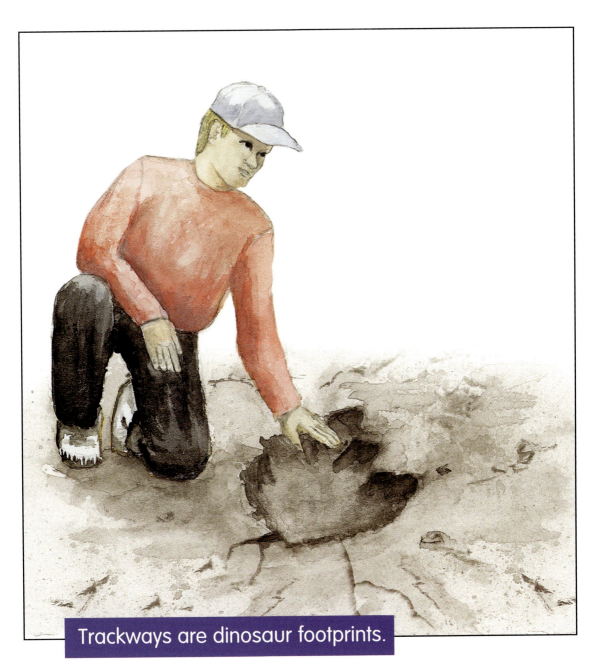

Trackways are dinosaur footprints.

Where Are They Today?

Smithsonian National Museum of Natural History
10th Street and Constitution Avenue
Washington, D.C. 20560
www.nmnh.si.edu/paleo/dino

American Museum of Natural History
Central Park West at 79th Street
New York, NY 10024
www.amnh.org

Royal Tyrrell Museum of Paleontology
Box 7500
Drumheller, Alberta T0J 0Y0 Canada
www.tyrrellmuseum.com

ANKYLOSAURUS

NAME MEANS	Fused Lizard
DIET	Plants
WEIGHT	10,000 pounds (4,536 kg)
HEIGHT	4 feet (1 m)
TIME	Late Cretaceous Period
ANOTHER ANKYLOSAUR	Edmontonia
SPECIAL FEATURE	Club tail
FOSSILS FOUND	USA—Montana Canada—Alberta

The Ankylosaurus lived 70 million years ago.

First humans appeared 1.6 million years ago.

Triassic Period	Jurassic Period	Cretaceous Period	Tertiary Period
245 Million years ago	208 Million years ago	144 Million years ago	65 Million years ago

Mesozoic Era • Cenozoic Era

FUN DINOSAUR WEB SITES

Dinosaurs
www.cfsd.k12.az.us/~tchrpg/Claudia/Ank.html
Designed for young children, this site offers fun activities and details on the Ankylosaurus's behavior and habitat.

Zoom Dinosaurs
www.enchantedlearning.com/subject/dinosaurs/dinos/Ankylosaurus.shtml
Read about how smart the Ankylosaurus was and how it walked.

BBC Online – Walking with Dinosaurs
www.bbc.co.uk/dinosaurs/fact_files/volcanic/ankylosaurus.shtml
Learn about the discovery of the Ankylosaurus at this informative site.

IMPORTANT WORDS

ankylosaur dinosaurs with thick, bony plates on their backs.

armor an outside covering that keeps what is inside safe.

continent one of the seven large land masses on earth.

Cretaceous period a period of time that happened 144-65 million years ago.

dinosaur reptiles that lived on the land 248-65 million years ago.

fossil remains of very old animals and plants.

frill a protective plate on the back of a triceratops's head.

paleontologist someone who studies plants and animals from the past.

Index

ankylosaur, **22-25, 29**

ankylosaurid, **24**

armor, **10, 14, 20-22**

beak, **16**

Brown, Barnum, **26**

Canada, **13, 29**

club tail, **8, 21, 24, 25, 29**

continent, **12**

Cretaceous period, **4, 12, 13, 29**

Edmontonia, **22, 23, 25, 29**

fossil, **26, 29**

frill, **14**

horn, **14, 22**

nodosaurid, **25**

North America, **12, 13**

Panoplosaurus, **22, 23, 24, 25**

plates, **10, 11**

South America, **12**

Sucre, Bolivia, **26**

trackways, **26, 27**

Triceratops, **14, 15**

Tyrannosaurus rex, **18, 19, 21**

United States, **13, 29**